HEELS ON STEEL

HEELS ON STEEL

a play in Three Acts

Ope Dara

Copyright ©2018 Ope Dara

ISBN: 978-978-966-924-0

All rights reserved.
No part of this book may be reproduced, distributed, stored in a retrieval system, or transmitted, in any form or by any means, electronic, electrostatic, magnetic tape, mechanical, photocopying, recording, or otherwise without prior written permission from the Publisher. For information about permission to reproduce selections from this book, write to info@wrr.ng

National Library of Nigeria Cataloguing-in-Publication Data

Cover Design: Akila Jibrin

Printed and Published in Nigeria by:
Words Rhymes & Rhythm Limited
Suite C309, Global Plaza Plot 366, Obafemi Awolowo Way, Jabi District, Abuja, Nigeria.
08169027757, 08060109295
www.wrr.ng

DEDICATION

To Clement Dara and Stella Dara

My igi leyin ogba[1]

CAST OF CHARACTERS

CHIEF ADELEKE: A man in his mid-fifties, Abike's husband

ABIKE: A feisty woman in her late forties, Chief Adeleke's wife

JAMES & EVELYN: Teenagers, children of Adeleke and Abike

DRIVER: The Adelekes' chauffer

CALLER (Oredolu Ajayi): Chief Adeleke's friend

BOLANLE: Abike's younger sister

MAMA: Abike's Mother

MRS AJANAKU: Chief Adeleke's acquaintance

DR.: Chief Adeleke's friend

Act I

Scene 1

The scene opens in Chief Adeleke's residence in Ondo, a state in south-western Nigeria.
It is early in the morning at about 7:00 AM in the Adelekes' sitting room which is tastefully furnished with modern day furniture. The electronics are large and there are two expensive paintings on the wall. Evelyn Adeleke, a young lady in her late teens is giggling to herself as she reads from a piece of paper.

(Enter James)

JAMES: (Affectionately) My sweet sister is giggling, I can tell someone had a beautiful night rest. Good morning, big sister.

EVELYN: (Smiling) Morning James, how was your night? (She laughs).

JAMES: Fabulous! What is the cause of this your undiluted happiness this morning? Did something happen in your dreams?

EVELYN: Nothing happened o. It's just this poem I'm reading. I found it on Daddy's table. It is one of his poems. This one is about mum. You should hear it. (Clears her throat)

(Starts reading) The title is...

MY WOMAN IS EGALITARIAN

When I professed my love for her
She said she was egalitarian and wouldn't wear aprons
I thought she was just an alpha-lady
And I caused no further confrontation
For I thought we were in collusion – body and soul

But her quest for equality detained my masculinity
She appointed herself as my supposed equal
Funny! Her claim of equality is that of insanity

My woman is equal to a man
Yet, she calls me to come kill wall-geckos
Oh! She screams when she sees rats in the home
Her equality is insane, for I pay all the bills
She remembers to call me to lift heavy luggage
And shoulders her emotional baggage as well

She hoots, when I don't help in cleaning up dishes
Yes she lays around in joy, spending my riches
Always holding my hands at public functions
Sharing my fame, yet refusing to bear my name

When she's crying her expectation of me is high
My shirt, a handkerchief, my shoulder, her pillow
My mouth must whisper sweet things of course!

It is romantic to always open the door

*For her entries and exits
She says it is 'very unromantic!'
But is it unprofessional to do same for me?*

*My woman is an ardent believer
That a man must not cry. Only women can
A man must learn, how to man up his own tears
To prevent them from falling
I tell you, my woman is a confused being
And, I am laughing out loud.*

JAMES: (Laughing) Jeez! Daddy is right o. I really need to see mum's reply.

(The sound of shouting and foul language reaches them from off stage. They look at each other.)

(Enter Chief and Abike arguing)

CHIEF: (Angry) It is quite obvious that you've lost all sense of propriety. What will it cost you as a woman to prepare my meals? I have provided gas cooker, potable water, machine for pounding yam and the likes to help you with these tasks. But, no, you went ahead to bring a grown man as chef to this house! Remind me how old the man is again? Forty? I pity you woman, you better correct your ways!

ABIKE: (Scornful) I don't know when you will tire for this argument. I am equal to you. Asking me to cook, when we can afford a chef. Or expecting me to do the chores while you laze around is no longer going to happen in this house. It is an effrontery I will no longer condone! Well, for your information, the chef I just brought in will oversee all the cooking.

CHIEF: (Heaves a sigh) How come, after all these years, you just suddenly realize that it is an outdated and useless culture to expect a wife to cook meals for her husband? I bet, you'll regret this, I promise you.

(He stomps out)

EVELYN: What is it again, mum?

JAMES: It's not good the way you spoke to dad, mum. That was harsh.

ABIKE: No, I wasn't harsh, son. Your father wants to continue to treat me like a common house help in this house. I allowed it in the past, but it will not happen anymore. Why does he think I have to be the one to cook for him, when we can afford to hire a help to do it? If he doesn't want a help, then we should all be in the kitchen cooking together because we are all humans and cooking isn't linked with the vagina. Don't we all eat...?

EVELYN: (Mouth agape) Ah, Mum! It is okay, just calm down, everything is going to be alright.

ABIKE: (Rolls her eyes) Your father disrespected me, and you are asking me to calm...?

JAMES: (Cuts in) But mum, you talked back at dad and...

ABIKE: (Voice raised) And so what? James, will you ever learn anything at all? Listen to me! You mustn't treat your future wife the way your father is treating me! You must know that a man and a woman are equal. And you Evelyn, like I've always told you, you're created to be equal to a man. You are not his subordinate.

JAMES & EVELYN: Yes, mum!
(Simultaneously)

ABIKE: Ehen, what was it you said you wanted to tell me the other time?

EVELYN: (Hesitant) Maybe we should talk about it later. You don't seem to be in a good mood now, and we wanted to ask some favors (grimaces, expecting an outburst from her mother.)

ABIKE: (Smiles) No, go ahead and tell me. (Holds Evelyn's hand) I am no longer angry. It is your dad I was angry at, not you.

EVELYN: I wanted to tell you to ask dad to let me go and finish my education abroad. Most of my friends and even our neighbors' kids are all abroad, even the ones I did better than at school. I am tired of staying in this miserable country. (Makes a sad face.)

JAMES: Me, I just want a car for my sixteenth birthday. All my mates got cars when they were much younger.

ABIKE: Is that all? (Hisses) So that is what you wanted to tell me and you were acting so strangely. Children, your wishes are my commands. It is done!

JAMES: Oh mum! That is my momma! You are my one and only civilized momma! (Dances shaku shaku) You're the best mum in the world.

EVELYN: Mum, you're my world (hugs her mother). I am proud to be your daughter!

ABIKE: See, children, I will always want the best for you. If not for your father, I would have gotten you these things since, long before you even asked for them. What is a car? Why shouldn't I want my daughter to study abroad? Isn't that the only way to ensure you can measure up with your male counterparts?

BOTH: Thank you.

ABIKE: So can I go out now?

BOTH: Yes. (They laugh.)

(Slowly, lights fade)

Scene 2

Chief Adeleke is seated at the dining table reading a newspaper. There is a bottle of water and a half filled glass on the table. He has just finished eating.

CHIEF: My God! Where is this country going to? What is this yeye government doing to end this Boko Haram nonsense? (He sips from the glass). They keep killing innocent people like flies

(Enter Abike with an open book in her hand. She sits on one of the chairs and faces him with a smug look on her face)

ABIKE: Good afternoon, Chief.

CHIEF: Afternoon. (Hesitantly)

ABIKE: Well, as a 'good wife' (She drags the 'Good wife part for emphasis) I came to discuss our children's interests with you. I am bringing it to you, the way good women do in the olden days would take theirs to their husbands, our own forefathers...

CHIEF: (Curtly) Please go straight to the point and stop the drama!

ABIKE: (Sarcastic) You don't want me to be a good wife anymore? Anyway, James wants a car for his birthday and Evelyn wants to continue her education abroad. They both deserve it.

CHIEF: James?! (He drops the newspaper) So James wants to drive a car? Interesting. Where is he? Let him come and tell me what he wants to do with a car. James! James! (He shouts louder). James!

JAMES: (Shouts from off stage) Dad, I am here.

(Enter James. He is jittery.)

CHIEF: James, I learnt you want a car.

JAMES: Yes, dad. (He looks down)

CHIEF: What for? You this lazy boy.

JAMES: (He grumbles before answering) Nothing! Just felt it's a necessity.

CHIEF: (Laughs) I agree with you. It is a necessity. But let me make something clear to you, even when and if you gain admission into the university, I won't buy you a car. (Raises his voice) Listen very well... if you think you need a car, work very hard at your studies, so that you can become great in life, and then you will be able to afford as many cars as possible with your...

ABIKE: (Cuts in) Chief, don't be so hard. *Ahn ahn,* he is your son! How much is a car that you won't buy for him?

CHIEF: I have said my own. (He picks up his newspaper and continues reading)

ABIKE: Well, if you will not buy the car, I will! (She turns to James). Don't mind your father, he's just pulling your legs. You will get the car.

CHIEF: (Annoyed) Do you see what you're doing? You are antagonizing me before my children. You are damaging him.

ABIKE: (Struggling to remain calm) No, I am not. I am only helping you adjust and correct what you're doing wrong. That is all.

CHIEF: Well, the ball is in your court, you can play it any how you like. But, I warn you, do not damage the lives of my children. Some children are hungry and this small boy is here demanding for a car. (Gives James a stern look) Get out of here... It is because you have more than enough in your stomach and...

(Exit James)

ABIKE: We have money. Why do we have to behave like poor people, Chief? (Chief does not answer) Anyway, what about Evelyn?

CHIEF: (Continues reading) Evelyn is going nowhere. I can't believe you're really suggesting she goes abroad after failing WAEC and NECO exams last year due to her lack of focus. If her life is such a mess while she is under us, what will become of her abroad?

ABIKE: (Laughing) You're so archaic, Chief! She will live in a hostel and the quality of education over there can't be compared to the one we have here in this country. How are we sure her WAEC and NECO exams were properly marked last year. People over there don't make things hard for their students like here.

CHIEF: (Angry) Is it a child who can't sit down, focus and study here in Nigeria that should be sent abroad? Woman! Where is your sense of reasoning? You're toying with the lives of these children.

ABIKE: (Half apologetic and half disdainful) Ok... Hmmm... But, my children have joy in what I do for them. You are the one they see as a devil in this house. Chief, most of our friends have their children abroad. Why can't we do the same when we can afford it? Is it only my children that must study in this miserable country? I am even ashamed.

CHIEF: (Cuts in) If my children dislike my actions, that is because, I've been painted as a devil by you. The Bible says a wise woman builds...

ABIKE: (She gets up angrily) Please, please if you want to say something, just say it, instead of quoting the Bible. Why deliberately put so much unnecessary pressure on women? (Mimicking Chief) Woman, submit to your husband... A wise woman builds her house... Woman this, woman that. I am beginning to think that the Bible needs a revised edition. It is this Bible that you all use to blame women for everything. No wonder there was not even a single woman among the twelve Disciples.

CHIEF: (Shocked) May God forgive you.

ABIKE: Stop being sanctimonious. Since we already have Old Testament & New Testament, I think we should have the Modern or Newer Testament that recognizes gender equality.

CHIEF: (Sniggers) Is it women that behave like you are doing now that Jesus should have made into disciples?

ABIKE: (Flares up) Please calm down, since the responsibilities for discipleship is too much for a woman, well, I can categorically say the responsibility of cooking and domestic chores is too much for me, and I can't do them anymore without you assisting me anytime the children are in school. (Hisses)

CHIEF: Why are you bringing that up again? You are not satisfied with bringing a grown up man with children to cook for you? God will have mercy upon you, dear. It is your duty, I am the man of this house, not you.

ABIKE: You are the one who needs the mercy of God more, because you don't talk about me breaking your ego anytime I contribute financially. Later you will claim that you were made to be the breadwinner, while I stay at home. But I still work and you say we can't be equal. No way!

CHIEF: Well, I have made my stance clear on this your thoughtless pampering on our kids. There will be no car and no one is going abroad. That is final. (He resumes reading his newspaper). I am in no mood to argue with you about finances, because there are millions of working class women who still manage the home front without claiming equality with men. So, you're not special.

ABIKE: (Mocking) And I have made it clear that my will and opinion in this house matters just as much as yours.

(Curtain closes)

Scene 3

Curtains open to reveal a bedroom in the Adelekes' residence. Evelyn is packing her bags. It has been a couple of months since her parents fought over her desire to travel.

JAMES: (Entering) Sister, I am going to miss you when you go. Now I wish I had asked to go with you, because this house will be freaking boring without you.

EVELYN: (Pauses to smile at him) You know I am going to miss you too. But don't worry, I will make sure we video call as often as I can. (Resumes packing) I can't wait to be abroad mehn!

JAMES: I trust you... As for me, I can't wait for my birthday to come so I can cruise the car mum will buy for me.

(Enter Abike)

ABIKE: Evelyn, make sure you pack a smaller bag with some clothes separately for this week.

EVELYN: This week? (Worried) Why should I pack clothes for this week? I don't get, mum.

ABIKE: Well, you know your father is not in support of you travelling from the start. In fact, I don't want you to be here when he comes back from the office today. You will spend the week at Bolanle's place because I sense that this week is going to be one hell of a war between your father and me. And I don't want you to be caught in the crossfire since you will be travelling next week.

EVELYN: I get it now. I'm done packing.

ABIKE: Take your bags to the car (James and Evelyn exit the room carrying the bags. She sits on the bed) Chief, when you come back to this house we will see who holds the power. (Faces the audience) Please, who really should hold power in this house? Is it my overtly traditional Chief with his antiquated ways of thinking or my humble self with my civilized ways? (Preens). The fire of civilization must keep burning in me and it can never be quenched. My opinions must count in this house.

(Slowly lights fade)

Scene 4

Dark room. When light appears, Abike is seated cross-legged in the room. Somi's Lady Revisited plays loudly on repeat.

(Enter James)

ABIKE: Where have you been since? Did you go with your sister?

JAMES: (Nods his head in the affirmative) I decided to go with her because I wanted to spend as much time with her as I can before she goes.

ABIKE: (Smiles) Call me the driver.

(Exit James. Few minutes later, the driver enters)

DRIVER: Madam, small Oga you call me?

ABIKE: Yes, I did. (Dismissively) If my husband asks you of Evelyn's whereabouts, just pretend not to know anything, else, I will sack you, and no amount of begging will change it.

DRIVER: (Laughing) Madam, me no fit disobey you oh. I take my grandfather head beg you. I swear, Madam, na u be my only number one oga for this house now.

Madam, for this street sef, every person dey respect you pass Margaret Thatcher, even sef pass Obama. No be lie. Madam, you know wetin dem dey take call you for street? Na "mama for her husband" na wetin dem dey call you and...

ABIKE: (Screaming at him) Will you shut up? Who asked you to recite Genesis to Revelations? Fool! Illiterate bombastic element! Get out of here.

DRIVER: (Pleading) Abeg madam... No vex, no be my fault, na beans wey I chop this morning dey make me misbehave.

ABIKE: Just go!

(Exit Driver)

Look at this foolish man. I asked him to do one simple task and he is delivering a drunken speech. What nonsense! (She resumes nodding her head to the music)

(Chief Adeleke enters, carrying a package.)

CHIEF: Afternoon, dear.

ABIKE: Afternoon, Chief.

CHIEF: Where is Evelyn? I got her some books. (Picks the DVD remote and lowers the volume of the music)

ABIKE: Evelyn? (Casually) By now she should be arranging her things in Los Angeles.

CHIEF: I'm not in the mood for joking around. Where is she? (Shocked) Evelyn! Evelyn! Woman, where is Evelyn? (Goes out hurriedly and comes back few minutes later) Her door is locked. Where is my daughter, woman? James! James! Woman!

ABIKE: I wasn't speaking French earlier on, Chief. I told you she has gone to the US. Did you think I was joking when I said I would send her abroad singlehandedly if you do not do it yourself?

CHIEF: (Stammering) And you thought it was a good idea to do it without telling me? Is this what you have become?

ABIKE: This is not what I have become. This is what you have made me into. (Calmly) Did you think that you can just keep dictating things to me forever? I am tired! Why it that a man's 'No' is 'No' and his 'Yes' is 'Yes' when he says so. But for women, it is whatever a man says that becomes their yes. We are not your subjects. I am your wife. I want my 'No' and my 'Yes' to stand!

CHIEF: (Pointing a finger at her) Is this how your so called fire of civilization burns? You want to burn this family to ashes? Now, tell me, where is Evelyn? Because if you don't tell me where my daughter is, I tell you, you'll rot in jail.

ABIKE: (Indifferently) Jail? Isn't she my daughter too? You know I am not intimidated by you, Chief. I am a Barrister, even though you destroyed my career many years ago, I am still sound up here. You know I never lost a case when I practiced (Gives a sly grin).

CHIEF: (Fuming) I can't believe you sent my daughter abroad without my consent simply because you have money.

ABIKE: (Exasperated) You are not angry I sent her abroad. You are angry I did not secure your approval. You want to control me like your children. Well I am not one of your subjects I am a woman, a full human being like you. (She turns on the volume of the music and dances mockingly). Evelyn has gotten what she wants. Stop worrying. Come and dance with me.

CHIEF: This is not over. You will see!

ABIKE: What do you think you have that I do not have? Is it money? Even your overhyped 'Chief' title, I can get one if I want! I will attend a function with you and they will keep saying "Chief and Chief Mrs. Adeleke" as if I don't have a name as well. I am not Mrs. Adeleke, I am Abike Jaiyeola, MS Abike Jaiyeola. Yes.

(Chief storms out angrily)

(Abike talking to the audience). Tell me, people, have I done wrong to demand that I have an equal say in the affairs of this house? When I married this man, he was a small businessman and I was a vibrant lawyer, winning cases. As a dutiful wife, I sacrificed my career to be a mother and dutiful wife as tradition expected of me. If I had continued my practice, perhaps I would be defeating Falana in court now, but I am here. We women will sacrifice our bodies and lives for our families and yet we won't get as much respect as their sex-slave secretaries. Nonsense! (Increases the volume of the music again and dances off stage.

(Curtain closes slowly)

Scene 5

Somewhere in the Adelekes' residence. Chief is seated alone reading a newspaper. Driver walks by carrying a bucket. He sees Chief and stops.

DRIVER: Ah! Oga, good evening. I dey hail you oh!

(Abike appears behind Chief. She gives the driver a knowing look before exiting)

CHIEF: Ehen, I was even looking for you. (Almost whispering) So... you drove Evelyn to the airport today... When?

DRIVER: (Acting Confused) Airport? Evelyn? I no sabi wetin you dey talk o, Oga.

CHIEF: Hmmm. (Strokes his beard) You can go!

DRIVER: Okay, Oga. (Walks off stage humming a traditional tune)

(Chief Adeleke's phone rings. He picks the call)

CHIEF: Oredolu Ajayi! Ore mi Ajayi! Omo ekun! Longest time! So you remember me today. Too much money has made you to forget your childhood friend abi. Ajayisco!

CALLER: Ore mi, don't try to escape. Is it not you that forgot me? You did not pick nor return my last call. Anyway, how are you doing over there in Naija?

CHIEF: (Heaves a sigh) We're doing fine o. How is Mama Bimpe and the children and the London weather?

CALLER: We are not doing badly. A dupe. Mama Bimpe always asks after you. And how is your civilized wife? I still haven't gotten over the fact that she almost stabbed me the last time I visited just because I said we might get you another wife soon.

CHIEF: My friend, (Grunts) I won't deceive you, things are worsening.

CALLER: Ore mi, you know you caused this yourself. I mean, you should have married a second wife, or pretended to be at least interested in another woman. It would put that woman in her place. I swear, she would have changed.

CHIEF: (Laughing hysterically) You think I've not done that? Ooh, let me tell you what has happened these past two months. I pretended to be interested in my secretary at work, showing my wife clues to make her jealous and behave. Instead of calming down, she brought down fire and brimstone.

CALLER: What did she do this time around? I hope she didn't harm your secretary?

CHIEF: Not at all. She was quiet about it initially, until her lawyer brought me a divorce notice. My wife wanted a divorce! I don't understand that woman at all.

CALLER: (Angry) Then, divorce her! To hell with her! What are you waiting for? You're behaving like a weakling, my friend. When did you become this way?

CHIEF: (In a low voice) Come on, calm down, you know... I am doing all these simply because I love my wife, I really do. You can't just get it. I fell in love with my wife, you know.

CALLER: (In disbelief) Oh! You're sounding like a weakling again. Does a man eat love? Is 'love' food? A man wants sex, children and submissiveness not love. My friend, I am afraid, I think you are too soft for this woman. If it were me, I would have dealt with her. I am yet to see a woman that would try such with me, an

Akoko man like myself. When I talk to my wife Mama Bimpe, she dares not talk back to me at all, otherwise she's dead.

CHIEF: (Trying to change the topic) So, how is business?

CALLER: (Not satisfied) Don't try changing the topic. What are you going to do about your cantankerous wife? (Pauses) Well, I intend to marry a younger wife myself.

CHIEF: (Surprised) You must be joking.

CALLER: Says who? (Laughs) The fact that I am in London doesn't mean I have to...

CHIEF: (Interrupts) If you marry another wife, then we cease to be friends.

CALLER: (Angry) Abi ori e daru ni. What are you talking about? In fact, you are annoying me. Weak man! Call me when you divorce your silly wife. (Call ends)

CHIEF: (Heaves a sigh) Ajayi, you want a younger woman! This man is mean o! What will happen to Mama Bimpe! Is this how this fool will repay this woman?

(Curtain closes)

Scene 6

Abike Jaiyeola comes out from a shopping mall. She walks towards her car, holding her car keys and a bunch of shopping bags. She stops when she hears her name from off stage.

VOICE: Abike, Mrs. Adeleke.

ABIKE: Who could that be? (She drops her bag and looks in the direction of the source of the voice.)

CHIEF MRS. AJANAKU: (Emerges from a corner) Oh... Chief Mrs. Adeleke, quite an age. How is Chief doing?

ABIKE: (Politely but firmly) Good day, Madam. Please, I will appreciate it if you can call me Abike Jaiyeola, not Chief Mrs. Adeleke.

CHIEF MRS. AJANAKU: (Looks at her queerly) Really? When did it happen? I mean the divorce... Eeyah!

ABIKE: (Flares up) Madam! Are you sure you're alright! Who divorced who? What is hard to comprehend in what I just said? Does the fact that I choose to bear my name, rather than my husband's, or that I rejected your traditional title, mean that I am now divorced?

CHIEF MRS. AJANAKU: (Sarcastically) Ooh... Abike, so this gist about your madness is true. You're a foolish woman o!

(Abike tries to leave but Mrs. Ajanaku stands in her path, staring at her)

ABIKE: Are you mentally stable at all?

CHIEF MRS. AJANAKU: You are the one who needs mental stability M-R-S A-DE-L-E-K-E. That is your name! You need some sanity and I will dish it to you whether you like it or not (She snatches Abike's car key). We won't leave here until I talk some sense into your head. You want to discard your husband's name like a used rag abi? What an abomination! It is unheard of in our culture. In fact, it is a slap on the ideologies of our forefathers. Don't you know a woman's husband is her Lord? Did your mother forget to instill that in you when you were young? Where did you get that madness about not bearing your husband's name from? Ehhh...

(A small crowd gathers around them)

ABIKE: (Fuming) Madam! You are a big fool (Slaps her and pushes her to the ground. Her car key drops. She picks it up and enters her car.

CHIEF MRS. AJANAKU: See her witch legs! Witchcraft runs in your blood! (She gets on her feet and dusts herself) Witch! No wonder your father died early, you mother must have killed him just as you want to kill your husband now. Wiiiiiittttttcccchhh!

ABIKE: (Turns back to face her) I don't blame you. Your problem is poverty of pocket and mind. Next time, buffoon, learn how to mind your business.

(She clicks her tongue and leaves)

CHIEF MRS. AJANAKU: (Claps in mockery) Witch! You will be kicked out of your husband's house! Mark my words!

(Enter security man)

SECURITY MAN: (Authoritatively) Madam, please, you are disturbing the peace.

CHIEF MRS. AJANAKU: (Hisses) Who is this one talking to? (She hisses again and walks off stage). Please leave, you are causing a scene.

(The crowd disperses gradually as curtain closes)

Act II

Scene 1

The scene opens in a well-furnished sitting room. Bolanle is mopping the floor.

(Enter Evelyn.)

EVELYN: Well done, Aunty.

BOLANLE: Thanks. How are you?

EVELYN: (Takes a seat) I am fine. But Aunty, why are you always working? Why can't you just get a maid?

BOLANLE: (Laughs) Maid? For what? I stay here alone, so the chores are not too much for me. Now that you are here, you can help me out as well.

EVELYN: Aunty (Bites her lips), something has been bothering me for a while.

BOLANLE: (Stops mopping) What is it, dear?

EVELYN: Do you believe in gender equality?

BOLANLE: (Confused) Do I believe in gender equality? Or am I a supporter of the ideology?

EVELYN: Both. Are you a supporter?

BOLANLE: (Laughs again). Hmm, I see your mother has been feeding you with her ideologies. See, my sister is not entirely right. Her own version of gender equality is even going above the word of God. In the Bible, God says, the wife should submit to the husband, and even in our culture, as Africans, it is an abomination. I mean gender equality itself as an idea.

EVELYN: (Curious) Mum believes that, man made culture, and as humans, we can decide what to see as culture and what not to see as culture, and that shows that gender equality can become our new culture. One day, she told me that gender equality is similar to where someone is a doctor while another is a pharmacist and they are both vital to the medical profession without one being considered superior.

BOLANLE: (Shakes her head) *Ah, o ma se o!* Why is your mother like this? Is she smarter than God who created men and women and gave them different roles? (Her phone rings) Excuse me, dear. (She picks it up). Hello... I am doing fine. Chief, this one that you remember me today… Hope you aren't trying to steal Evelyn from me…

EVELYN: (Trying to interrupt Bolanle) Aunty… Ermh… Aunty…

BOLANLE: Yes of course, Evelyn is here! She came to spend the week. Didn't know? (She looks at Evelyn). Really? No problem. You will meet her here. Ok, I will be waiting. Take care, sir. (She cuts the call and faces Evelyn). You! Now! Start talking… So, your father didn't know you are here?

EVELYN: (Fidgeting) Aunty, I am so sorry. (She narrates all that happened truthfully)

BOLANLE: (Angry) Your mother never ceases to amaze me. Is this equality or stupidity? So, you both lied to me. So, I am not even worthy of knowing the truth, but you could manipulate me? How could your mother be so disrespectful to your father like that? And you! I pity you if you take after her.

EVELYN: Aunty…

BOLANLE: I am a little ashamed that your mother is my sister. What more rubbish has she been teaching you?

EVELYN: Erm, Aunty...

BOLANLE: Don't Aunty me! Are you that desperate to travel abroad? Even if your mother advised you wrongly, can't you behave maturely for once? You failed your exams terribly, so much that even your mum complains. Despite all these, you want to abscond overseas?

EVELYN: It's not like that. (Starts sobbing)

BOLANLE: This place isn't a time for tears, dear. Wipe away your tears! You have to make a decision because you are at a crossroad. I can only tell you that your mum's stand on gender equality is extreme and you should not use that as an advantage to travel abroad without your father's consent.

EVELYN: (In tears) Aunty, I am confused.

BOLANLE: Dear, there is nothing to be confused about, just that sex equality, as your mother pursues it, is absurd. It will only lead to problems in marriages. I must salute your father for being able to stay faithful, because it will be tough to stay with a woman who has been running the affairs of the home like this. I wonder why your father has not reported her to mama and papa.

EVELYN: Mummy will not be moved even if she were reported. Her mind is made up on this matter.

BOLANLE: You're right, my dear. Your mother has been talking about this equality thing since when we were teenagers. She was studying for her first degree at the university then. It was when she met one English writer named Charlie Brendett, that she became radical. Your mother used to read Brendett's books and attend her workshops. We never imagined it would ever get this bad.

EVELYN: (Cuts in) Now I understand better...

BOLANLE: What do you understand?

EVELYN: Aunty, mum only became very aggressive last year after she returned from a trip to the UK. I think she went for that Brendette woman's seminar, because she returned with some pamphlets and books with that name. Things have not been the same since then…

BOLANLE: (Sarcastic) Charlie Brendett again! She's still alive? I wonder how many homes she has ruined.

EVELYN: Mum has been reading the woman's books, especially one titled "The Winning Woman". She gave me to read too. That books changed her o. It was after that period that she told dad that she wouldn't be doing the cooking alone anymore because it is not the duty of a woman to cook. She hired a cook. Later, she said she doesn't want to be addressed with daddy's name, but her own maiden names. She particularly said she should be addressed as Ms., not Mrs.

BOLANLE: Which one is MS again?

EVELYN: It is used for both married and unmarried females.

BOLANLE: See, your husband is the head while you are the neck…

EVELYN: (Cuts in) No o… (Laughing) Mum doesn't believe in that. She even gave it a name: Egali… Egalitarian Nonsensical.

She said that it is either you're equal to somebody or you're not.

BOLANLE: (Hesitant) Well... hmm.... your mother has been feeding you a lot of rubbish, my dear. Since your father isn't doing anything to change the situation, I know what to do.

(Someone knocks)

Perhaps, it's your dad. Come in.

(Enter Chief Adeleke, carrying a briefcase)

EVELYN: Dad! Good afternoon, sir.

CHIEF: How are you doing?

EVELYN: I am fine.

(They both take a seat)

BOLANLE: (Curtseys) My Distinguished Honorable Chief, Chief Commander himself! Baba for everyone, what do I offer you? I have amala, rice...

CHIEF: I am okay, my dear. (Turns to Evelyn). So, here is the 'abroad' your mother sent you to Evelyn?

EVELYN: (Goes on her knees) Dad, I am very sorry. I am sorry for disobeying you.

CHIEF: Hmmm. It is okay, my princess. (Faces Bolanle) Thanks for taking care of my princess, and for letting me know she's here.

BOLANLE: You're welcome, Chief. (Pauses) But, Chief... you're taking my sister's case with levity oh, all these had been happening and you refused to let us know... Why don't you report her to mama and papa, so they can talk some sense into her head? (Goes on her knees) I am so sorry, Chief. This wasn't how we were trained as women. Please, forgive her... I promise to talk to her.

CHIEF: (In a cool voice) Thanks, Bolanle. But I decided not to report her to anyone. What if your parents were no more? Would I have reported her to their ghosts? So, don't tell mama and papa anything. I promise to resolve things amicably by myself, with God by my side. (Turns towards Evelyn) So, you still want to travel abroad?

EVELYN: Not any longer, dad.

CHIEF: (Affectionately) I am proud of you, my dear. I am ready to send you to any part of the world for quality education.

43

But I want you to have the requisite maturity and qualifications. I am just waiting to be sure of your readiness.

EVELYN: Dad, a trial will convince you.

(They burst into laughter)

CHIEF: I have to get going. I was on my way for a 12 noon meeting when I learnt you were here. (Gets up from his chair) By the way, will you be returning home today or would you prefer to spend more time with your aunt?

EVELYN: I think I...

BOLANLE: (Interrupts) She's staying oh! Why are you people being so possessive? She has barely spent two days here. Let her stay joor...

CHIEF: (Laughs) It is okay, she'll stay. Alright, take care.

EVELYN: Let me walk you to the car.

CHIEF: Thanks, Love.

(Exit Evelyn and Chief. Bolanle resumes cleaning)

(Curtain closes)

Scene 2

Later that day at the Adelekes' residence. James and Abike are seated in the sitting room. It is a day to his birthday.

ABIKE: (Teasing) James the birthday boy. Happy eighteenth birthday to you, my dear. You're getting old. (Laughs)

JAMES: Thank you, mum. I hope you remember what you promised me?

ABIKE: What did I promise you? Is it this? (Hands him a car key.) This is your key. Your car is parked in the garage. (James collects the key and jumps into her arms).

JAMES: (Excited) Oh! Mum, you're simply the best. I love you to the moon and back!

ABIKE: So when are your friends arriving for your party tomorrow?

JAMES: (Whispering) Mum, I am not celebrating it here.

ABIKE: (Pretending to be surprised) Why?

JAMES: The friends coming to grace my birthday are big boys and girls, I don't want them to come and be embarrassed by dad. He has already warned us about alcoholic drinks and loud music. How can we have fun like that?

ABIKE: So where do you intend using?

JAMES: Joseph's place.

ABIKE: Joseph... which Joseph?

JAMES: Joseph Asubiojo

ABIKE: Professor Asubiojo's son? It's okay. Just make sure you are a good boy. I need to go out for a bit. You'll tell me all about your plans when I return.

JAMES: Okay mum. Thank you again.

(Abike exits the stage)

JAMES: (Throws the key into the air and catches it.) Yes! Thank you, mother! Ah! Nike, Funmi, Belinda, you people will feel my swag.

(Enter Chief Adeleke. James does not notice his father's presence. He continues dancing around.)

JAMES: Ladies, you're in for a fun ride. I will show you that I am the baddest....

CHIEF: No, you won't! (James is startled) Now, hand over the key. (Stretches out his hand).

JAMES: (Rudely) For what!

CHIEF: What did you say? (Slaps him) I am your father! You will not talk to me that way! Give me the key?

JAMES: Daaad! (Sulking).

CHIEF: Unless you're a bastard, you will hand over that key right now!

JAMES: Why are you trying to ruin my joy? (Hands over the key)

CHIEF: (Sarcastic) Good boy! Now! Have your seat. (Points to the sofa)

(James angrily takes a seat)

If you're this rude to me now, what will happen later in life? Look, son, son, I pray you listen to whatever I tell you now so that you can categorically say that I tried my best whenever you look back.

(Enter Evelyn)

EVELYN: (Shouting) Happy birthday, brother! Good afternoon dad.

JAMES: (Gruffly) It's tomorrow *joor!*

CHIEF: How are you? Come join your brother, dear. (Evelyn sits). I was just telling your brother now that it is his duty as my son to be responsible. It is compulsory...

(Enter Abike)

ABIKE: (She is surprised to see the three together) What are you doing here, Evelyn? You have just two days... ehm...

EVELYN: This is my home, mum. (Sweetly) I guess I am always welcome. (Looks at her father with a telling smile)

ABIKE: What brought about this family meeting?

CHIEF: I took the car key from James.

ABIKE: (Frowns) The car I bought for him?

CHIEF: (Smiling) Oh yes! And now, I am lecturing him on how to live a responsible life. Isn't that interesting?

ABIKE: (Hisses and starts walking away) Really? Evelyn, come, I need to talk to you.

EVELYN: Mummy, wouldn't it be rude for me to leave here while Dad is still talking to me?

ABIKE: You called me rude, Evelyn!

EVELYN: No, mum. I'm just saying it would be improper to leave before dad is finished. Calling me away is rude as well.

CHIEF: (Firmly) Evelyn, stop! I won't have you speak to your mother that way.

EVELYN: No Dad, for once let me speak, please... if you want me to shut up forever, then no problem. (Turns to her mum) Mum, I love you very much, but please wake up and see how you're ruining this home. Isn't it ironic that you were angry that I disrespected just now, but it is what you do to dad almost very moment.

ABIKE: Me! (She is shocked) You're talking to me? You, Evelyn?

EVELYN: You keep shouting equality every time, but I want to know if we must disrespect people just to prove we are equal to them. Now let's assume gender egalitarianism is a right ideology, is MS Adeoye not practicing gender egalitarianism? Just look at the way she and her husband respect each other's opinions...

ABIKE: (Cuts in) Shut up! I won't have you lecture me. When did you get to this world? I am your mother! Gender egalitarianism is a social movement supporting the equality of both sexes in all aspects of public and private life. It specifically argues that legal and social restrictions on females must be removed in order to bring about such equality. Is that bad? Is it too much for a woman to want equal opportunity and respect? Is it? (She is almost in tears).

JAMES: (Sniggers) Mum, is that the definition from Civic Education textbook or dictionary?

ABIKE: Will you shut up there?! I know you all are still ignorant of what gender equality means so I will indulge you with some. Charlie Brendett said in her book "The Winning Woman" ...

CHIEF: (Interrupts) Yes of course! You must mention that book which has reshaped your life, a book that turned my wife from an angel to a cantankerous stranger. (Laughs) Abike, have you enjoyed this marriage since your gender equality declaration? Absolutely not! The same applies to me, because we've been fighting for superiority ever since. From your actions, all I can say is that gender equality is an ideology promoted by disobedient women in a bid to disrespect men. Tell me how many feminists with such ideologies have happy marriages?

ABIKE: (Defensively) A lot, my silly dear. Charlie Brendett is 70 years; she has been married for forty five years. Same goes for my friend Adeoye, Lily Beckham! Judy Augustus, Seyi Adedeji, this Nigerian female writer from the North, ehm Nana Abdul, and a host of others, too.

CHIEF: (Chuckles) Did you follow them home? How are you sure they're hundred percent about this ideology in terms of practice? Do they run their homes by what they write? (Inquisitive) I can boldly tell you that those who follow that ideology truthfully, and still have their marriages intact, are only successful because they're in the Western world! I am an African man, I can't allow such nonsense.

ABIKE: (Angrily) Oh! You see that as nonsense! It is nonsense because you're an African man? Shame on you then! You people don't always remember you're Africans when you wear westernized clothes, T-shirts, shoes, drive cars, but you always remember you're an African when you tell your wife it is her duty to pound yam... to cook meal, to even pretend not to see you when you cheat...

CHIEF: (Angry) Have I ever cheated on you?

ABIKE: How would I know? After all, I don't follow you everywhere, do I? There's that your secretary (she bats her eyelids disrespectfully). Anyway, I was speaking of African men generally.

CHIEF: Generalization is bad, dear. When speaking to me, be specific.

ABIKE: I will generalize! (Shouting) Because gender equality is a fight for all women! A fight we must win. Like the late Maya Angelou said, "Each time a woman stands up for herself without knowing it, possibly without claiming it, she stands up for all women." I don't like the way African men treat women, like mere possessions... like women should be superheroes to domestic chores... like a woman is created to serve a 'Majesty' called 'Man'.

CHIEF: (Half angry, half smiling) I told you to be specific, woman! Which way do you not like? Is it the fact that I buy you fanciful clothes and shoes any time I am out... the way I take care of you, the way I've always listened to your advice.

ABIKE: (Cuts in) You only do that before. Besides, I buy stuff like that for you too, it is not legendary. You're not the first man to do that and you won't be the last.

CHIEF: (Retorts) I stop doing those beautiful things since you're into this gender madness. Remember, I used to join you in the kitchen to cook before. Remember how I supported your every dreams. Remember how you would advise me and I would listen with rapt attention because I admired you... How I would wake you up in the morning with a beautiful text on your phone and how I would end it at night despite the fact that we are under the same roof. What else do you want, Abike?

(Knocking is heard off stage)

CHIEF: James, check who is at the door.

(Exit James)

ABIKE: I want equality! (Very loudly) I want equality! That is what I want! Is that all? Treat me like your equal and we will remain a happy couple. Why must you only dictate? Why should everything revolve around you men? You people say it is a man's world, but, if you don't treat me as your equal, I will take it myself! It is high time women started to believe they hold the power to say and be whatever they want to be. I don't mind championing that in this locality. Besides, you think all I've ever wanted is a romantic text and romantic date. Of course not, my silly dear, I am not some baby you give candy then take something valuable from. You talk about you cooking dinner, what's so special about that? Everyone eats and thus anyone should cook. Cooking isn't learnt from the vagina. It's not a genital feature of the female gender. So, stop hammering on that.

(Enter James with a large travelling bag. An aged woman follows behind him. Everyone greets as soon as they notice her presence)

CHIEF: Welcome, Mama! What a pleasant surprise! It's been quite a long while! Welcome. How is papa and everyone?

MAMA: Everyone is fine, my son? Evelyn, my Angel? How are you?

EVELYN: (Excited) I am fine oh... I am so glad to see you.

JAMES: Welcome, grandma. Tomorrow is my birthday!

MAMA: Eighteenth? (James nods). You're going to be a man tomorrow then. (Turns to Abike who is frowning, obviously unhappy to see her) Abike, you don't want to greet me? Anyway, what is it I have been hearing about you?

(Chief signals the kids to leave. Exit James and Evelyn)

I heard you stopped cooking for your husband, you dropped his name and you fight him every time. Is that how I brought you up? Tell me! You're bringing me shame in my old age.

CHIEF: (Sympathetically) Mama, please don't cry, it is okay.

MAMA: If not that your husband is a good man, by now, he should have thrown you out. How can you do this to him? Well, I have come to stay with you for some time, I will be spending a month here, and I won't be tolerating any nonsense from you at all.

ABIKE: (Defensively) But Mama, this is my matrimonial home.

(Chief's phone rings, he picks it up)

CHIEF: Hello Doc... (Smiling) How are you doing? My friend died? Which friend? I didn't hear anything about anyone dying. (Pauses) Oredolu? The same Oredolu? How? What happened? (Pauses) Ajayi now, husband to Mama Bimpe. (Screams) Yeh-yeh... Iku o! Iku o!

(Enter James and Evelyn)

CHIEF: What will become of Mama Bimpe and the children?!

EVELYN & JAMES: Dad, who died? (Simultaneously)

MAMA: (Scared) Who died, my son?

ABIKE: (Frightened) Chief, what is it?

CHIEF: Oh God! This is so sad, he still called me a week ago to discuss my marriage. He even told me his intention of marrying another wife, and I told him we would cease to be friends if he goes ahead to do so. (He puts the phone on speaker)

CALLER: Well… that is exactly what led to his death. He told his wife of his intention to take another wife. It didn't go well with her. They got into an argument and she stabbed him to death.

CHIEF: (Takes a deep breath) Hmmm… that is so sad. Doc, where is Mama Bimpe now?

CALLER: (Sarcastic) Are you seriously asking me that? She is in detention, of course!

CHIEF: Alright Doc., we will talk later. I need to make some arrangements.

CALLER: Alright, Chief. Extend my regards to your wife and children.

(Call ends)

CHIEF: God! (Shakes his head vigorously) This news is very disheartening. And I warned him o!

EVELYN: (Sadly) Take it easy dad.

MAMA: My God! What will not happen these days? So a wife stabbed her husband just because he wanted to take another wife. O ma se o! In our forefathers' days, they married as many wives as possible. No stabbing! No killing! No confrontations! But children of nowadays are doing lots of abominable things, imagine what this one, (Pointing to Abike) is doing to herself.

ABIKE: (Angry) Oh! (Sarcastic) Mama Bimpe's husband didn't obey their marriage vow, so... is she supposed to clap for him and not get angry? (Hissing) Though, I am not justifying the murder, how could Oredolu treat his wife like that? How could he? The woman laboured with him before he became rich. How dare he even think of another wife!

(Turns to the audience)

It is pathetic that men call women the weaker ones when men are truly the weaker ones! A man will cheat on his wife and she will be expected to forgive him, regardless of the number of time, whereas a woman can't even cheat on a man once. Since men refer to women as the weaker ones, aren't women supposed to be treated with care, dignity, respect? I tell you, a man who cheats on a woman has zero respect for her. And the society agrees that women are too emotional? Then how do you treat an emotional woman? Is it by cheating on her, disrespecting her? If that is it, I think men are the cause of women emotional problems. (Pointing) You men are the cause of your wives' murderous and suicidal thoughts.

CHIEF: You have come with your generalization again. (Mimicking) 'You men', I told you to be specific.

ABIKE: (Ignores him) I put it to you that men are weaker, they are too weak to forgive a cheating spouse! Some of them are afraid of the thought of their wives becoming richer. Indeed, men are generally weaklings.

MAMA: (Angrily) Abike! (Touching her tummy) I am your mother and I forbid you to continue this conversation. I am hungry, I want to eat pounded yam with egusi soup and goat meat... (Pauses) And you know I hate my food being prepared by maids.

ABIKE: (Frowns) Oh! Mama.

MAMA: Don't mama me! (Authoritatively) Go cook for me and your husband!

(Abike leaves the room while Chief smiles sheepishly)

(Curtain closes)

Act III

Scene 1

Curtain opens to reveal the Adelekes' kitchen. Abike is cooking. Mama is seated on a chair in one corner of the kitchen.

MAMA: My daughter, well done… This is how a good wife ought to be

ABIKE: (Angrily) Mama! This is my matrimonial home; you can't be here running things for me! How could you send my cook away without my consent?

MAMA: Please, shut up and cover your face in shame. You are not ashamed to have a full grown man as house help. How do you cope eating food from a man? *Oro buruku!* My own daughter is eating food prepared by men, neglecting her duties! You think if your mother-in-law and your father-in-law were here, you'll be trying all this nonsense? You think they would keep mute and watch you disrespect their son? Abike! I am telling you, as a mother who is overly concerned about you, that I am displeased. Do you even know you're disgracing me at all? Do you know how many times I've cried because of you? (Sobbing) Abike! You're my pride, please don't allow my enemies to mock me, they have already begun to do so... they talk of how you have charmed your husband... how you don't listen to him. Initially, I thought it was hearsay. Abike, it is true...

ABIKE: (Puts her hands on her shoulder) Mama, stop crying. Don't mind all those intellectual ignoramuses, Mama. They are merely intellectually unsound, no more than vegetable brains. Unlike them, I am educated, an intellectually fresh salad and...

MAMA: (Cuts in) And what Abike! You've disrespected all the teachings I gave you. (Beating her chest) Abike! What other women can be better role model than me, your mother? See the way I've kept my marriage of fifty years intact! Those women teaching you all forms of rubbish, are they wiser than me your mother? (Removes her scarf and touches her grey hair) My dear, not everything can be learnt from books or is it a crime I sent you to the university? You see! The fact that I am not a professor doesn't make me know less or less knowledgeable. I've seen a lot. You talk about being educated, isn't Mama Rhoda's daughter educated? She doesn't behave like you!

ABIKE: (Cuts in) But Mama, I am not doing anything wrong... I am just fighting for women's rights. Moreover, Mama, you don't compare me with a doormat... that literate illiterate... Don't even go there, Mama.

MAMA: No, my daughter. I know of women who speak on women empowerment, women who are championing campaigns against women abuse and domestic violence, and at every time speak against these vices. These women cook for their husbands, obey them and the likes. Do you have two heads?

ABIKE: But, Mama... gender equality is more important to make all these easy to fight for. When men see women as their equals rather than their subordinates, then they won't treat them like pieces of trash.

MAMA: (Angrily) Abike! You have the spirits of anger and stubbornness in you oh! How else do I talk to you to make you see reason for God's sake? (Sobbing) God knows I listened to my mother before her demise. Now! My own daughter won't listen to me! God, why! What is my offence?

ABIKE: (Downcast) Mama, I am sorry if I am hurting you. I...

MAMA: (Interrupts) Yes! You're hurting me! You're hurting your husband! In fact, your father isn't proud of your actions at all. Or you want me to call him and tell him of your stubbornness?

ABIKE: No, Mama. Please don't call Papa. We can both handle this issue now, Mama. We have both been discussing like intellectuals.

MAMA: And I've been discussing with you all this while, did you listen?

ABIKE: (Jovially) Mama, in Science, we have what we call hypothesis, evaluation, experiment and the likes. You can't just tell me something difficult and expect me to swallow it immediately. I've to digest it first, Mama.

MAMA: (Hisses) Too much of books is what is worrying you.

ABIKE: Mama, it is not too much of books. I have promised to reach out and empower women out there, to tell them it is not always their fault when their marriages fail. I want to tell a young girl that she has a voice! That everything about her shouldn't be based on sexuality! That no man should castigate a woman and make her feel inferior! That women are not superheroes and they should be allowed to make mistakes and learn from their mistakes without the society judging them. I don't want a woman to keep suffering and smiling in marriage, pretending that all is fine. I wonder why the society would go to the extent of telling a woman that her marriage failed because she didn't invest enough… when men are not held accountable for their obvious shortcomings as husbands.

MAMA: (Cuts in) Tell young women whatever you wish, I am not against you standing up for women… I am against this your equality with men.

ABIKE: (Sweetly) Mama, you're an old school, we're in a civilized era, Mama. How can I tell a woman she is this special without first telling her she is equal to a man; no superiority and no subordination? With gender equality I don't need to tell her she has a voice to do this and do that, because she already knows she is equal to a man and needs not take any order from him.

MAMA: (Takes a deep breath) I have said my bit. He who has ears, let him hear. I am still your mother.

ABIKE: Of course! You will forever be my mother. Sincerely, if you were a tunnel of birth, I will come through you a million times. (Jovially) You need to be slightly crazy in our world to be civilized, Mama. If you are not a little bit crazy, you're ancient.

MAMA: I would rather be ancient than astray.

(Mama walks out of the kitchen. Abike continues cooking. Enter Chief)

CHIEF: Wow! Nice aroma. (Laughing) I've so missed your cooking Abike.

(He gives her a bear hug from behind)

ABIKE: (Blushing) Really... You missed my cooking? The chef does a better job...

CHIEF: Not like you, dear. I am serious. (He kisses her) I brought you something. (He brings out a parcel and opens it)

ABIKE: Wow! I so love this. Come on, please put it on my neck! What are you waiting for?

CHIEF: Why not wait until you're done cooking, dear?

ABIKE: (Smiling) Alright?

CHIEF: So, how was your day? Any gist? Anything you want to tell your husband?

ABIKE: Well... (Smiles) You know Mrs. Bamidele? Well, she was caught today by her husband having sex with another married man in her shop. The husband went crazy and it was quite hilarious. (Laughs loud) I wonder what the husband will do with her.

CHIEF: (Laughs) Maybe her husband doesn't satisfy her in bed? Or maybe he isn't as romantic as I am?

ABIKE: (Giggling) Says who?

CHIEF: (Touching the parcel) Maybe I should just take this away then... since I am not romantic.

ABIKE: I know you won't try that (Chuckles). So, how was your own day?

CHIEF: (In a low voice) Tiresome! I'm beat down!

ABIKE: Eeeyah...

CHIEF: I fired someone today.

ABIKE: Really... Who? What was the offence?

CHIEF: (Smiling) Dear, one question at a time. It is my secretary o. You know she is fond of wearing provocative dresses and I have warned her severally about them. Today she tried to seduce me in my office. I had to give her the red card to prevent any unfortunate incident.

ABIKE: (Hugs him slyly) It is good for her! There are lots of graduates out there without jobs, and there she is, misbehaving. (Chuckles) Shame on her! Shame! A big time shame! Well, sweetheart, you did the very best thing. I am so proud of you.

CHIEF: (Playfully) Of course! I am the best husband in the world. I know in your next life, you'll marry me over and over again.

ABIKE: (Laughing) You're just too egoistic... but I like you like that (Kisses him) You're awesome.

(Enter James. He sees them and slowly exits)

ABIKE: Your son just saw us and quietly retreated. Funny boy...

CHIEF: Don't mind him. It is MY house, sorry, OUR house...

ABIKE: Hahahah, don't worry, we will finish this later. My food is burning. (She puts off the gas)

CHIEF: What can I help you with?

(Curtain closes slowly)

Scene 2

Scene is Evelyn's bedroom. She is reading a piece on the bed.

(Knocking.)

EVELYN: Yes? Come in

(Enter James)

JAMES: (Sits on the bed) This house is bubbling these days. All thanks to Mama.

EVELYN: (Cynically) Even though you don't have a car yet?

JAMES: (Retorts) Even though you're in Nigeria instead of U.S.A.

EVELYN: (Laughs) I choose not to be there anymore, I chose to listen to dad's advice.

JAMES: (Takes a deep breath) Hmm... Daddy's girl! Well, as for me, the least of my priority is getting a car for now. I just want to face my studies squarely.

EVELYN: (Sarcastic) Serious student.

JAMES: Oh! You can say that again. But I do have some fears... I hope that when Mama leaves this house, mum doesn't go back to her equator *wahala*.

EVELYN: Equator? (Laughing) I bet, she won't. Moreover, mum seems to love the attention she's getting from dad since their reunion.

JAMES: Well, if you say so. But, Evelyn, what is your take on the equality thing?

EVELYN: Well, I won't tell you whether I am a supporter of gender equality as an ideology or not, since I am still studying it. But I will categorically say that we Africans are not yet ready for it. It cannot work at this period in Africa. As a matter of fact, it is dead on arrival. It would take time for the ideology to be embraced here, but rather than preach gender equality, why not first speak of female empowerment? Speak or preach of female financial independence...

JAMES: (Cuts in) Exactly my point! Female empowerment is the way to go. Some women see the phrase 'gender equality' as an abomination. To them, they see it as you telling them to disobey the Bible or the Quran. So, in fighting for women's rights, female empowerment programmes should be encouraged, followed by social education programmes against abuse in marriages. As it is, the mode of pursuing this gender equality is only causing more chaos in already fragile marriages.

EVELYN: Yes, you're right. You see, gender equality is tempting. For instance, how come when a woman ends a relationship with a man, the society will say she broke up with him but when a man ends a relationship with a woman, the society will say she was 'used and dumped'?

JAMES: (Cuts in) Used and dumped? Does she become useless because she left him, or does she lose her self-worth simply because a relationship ended? Is she the only one worse off because the relationship ended? *Abeg*.

EVELYN: Exactly my point! Are women garbage that we use the term 'Dumped' for after having failed relationships? These are many salient points that give justification for the 'gender equality' movement, but the ideology is too immature for Africa. It will take time.

JAME: (Assertively) Such ideology can't be embraced in Africa by most men, and even women... at least not in this generation, especially here in this country with our religiosity.

EVELYN: But eventually it will... It is just a matter of time. For every ideology, there are people that are extreme about it, I mean the extremists, like mum. But even in all that rashness, there are some truths, many truths. Mum captured some of them in one of her poems. I saw it in a journal and copied it into my diary (Brings out a jotter from under her pillow) Read it. (Hands the jotter to James) It is a fantastic poem in support of gender equality.

JAMES: (Takes the jotter) What do we have here?

(Reads aloud)

I AM BOHEMIAN

This wall they said had been built –
A predecessor of my own birth
That this was how it was, a creed
And how it should be done

But I...
A foray of tomorrow's moon
Here comes the bohemian, me!
Daunting in the face of scrupulous customs

Standing shoulder shoo-in with men

They said I should make the pantry a home
The Apron, my regalia
Put a man's name on my head
And carry it everywhere I go
I was obliged to ask
The fate of my pretty name
And when I refused a man's name
They said, what is she?
They said, stay in the kitchen
Not to be heard, else I be damned

Some tradition will but fade
Their rays will soon be gone
Like daily washed Ankara
I am a lady!
I have no malady!
I must be heard like a man

I can entertain your brouhaha
My fellow menfolk
Who cried 'shut up'
You will watch me like a moon?
And make sense of my never dim light
Then shall your eyes see
I am bohemian
Too rigid for you

EVELYN: (Excited) And that is our beloved poet.

(Chief calls their names off stage)

EVELYN: We are wanted.

(Exit James and Evelyn)

Scene 3

Scene is the Adelekes' living room. Abike, Mama and Chief are talking in low voice. Soft traditional Yoruba music plays in the background.

(Enter James and Evelyn)

EVELYN: Daddy you called.

JAMES: Sir... (Sees Mama's luggage) Mama, I thought you said you will be spending a month with us?

MAMA: (Laughing) I actually did, but grandfather is missing me already. He has been calling me up and down as if I have travelled overseas.

EVELYN: (Frowning) Oh Mama! I am going to miss you. (Hugs her)

MAMA: I will miss everyone. (Turning to Abike) Dear, remember all we discussed.

ABIKE: I will never forget, Mama.

CHIEF: (Clears his throat) hmmm... Mama, thank you very much for everything. I am so grateful! You're a great mother indeed! Now! I know the importance of having good in-laws.

MAMA: (Happily) I should be the one to thank you, my son. You are a good son-in-law, too. May God bless you abundantly. Alright! I want to be on my way now.

(Chief, Abike and the children leave the stage then come back after some minutes)

ABIKE: What are we having for dinner?

EVELYN: (Jokingly) Mum, is the chef back?

ABIKE: (Pretending not to understand) Chef? What chef? You children should better meet me in the kitchen.

JAMES: (Teasing her) But I am a boy, mum!

ABIKE: Boys don't eat? Being a boy doesn't mean you shouldn't know how to cook because cooking skills are not assigned only to Homo sapiens with female genitalia.

JAMES: Ehen, mum has come again!

ABIKE: Children, (firmly) join Mrs. Adeleke in the kitchen.

EVELYN: Mrs. Adeleke? Since when?

CHIEF: (Cuts in) Since ever.

(They all burst into laughter)

(Curtain closes)

THE END

www.ingramcontent.com/pod-product-compliance
Lightning Source LLC
Chambersburg PA
CBHW051349040426
42453CB00007B/490